T0182564

THE TOP TEN

MOST DANGEROUS PLACES ON EARTH

whitestar·kids

LET'S GO!

**OUR PLANET IS FULL OF WONDERFUL NATURAL PLACES
THAT TAKE OUR BREATH AWAY. MANY, HOWEVER,
ALSO HIDE INCREDIBLE AND FEARSOME DANGERS...**

Extreme environmental conditions, aggressive animals, and
uncontrollable forces of nature can transform these seemingly
peaceful locations into terrifying places. If you enjoy a bit of risk,
join us on an adventure that will take you beyond your wildest
dreams. Check out our Top Ten and discover some of the most
terrifying places on earth, all of which should be visited with
extreme caution or avoided completely.

**WARNING!
THIS BOOK IS NOT FOR THE FAINT OF HEART!**

DANGEROUS
FEATURE

FUN FACT

Look for these symbols to discover surprising **FUN FACTS**
and find out which **DANGEROUS FEATURES** make these
TEN PLACES worthy of a spot on our list!

THE DANGER LEVEL WILL RISE FROM 10 UP TO THE TERRIFYING NUMBER 1

Hello! My name is Peggy, and I'm a homing pigeon. Thanks to my many travels, I have created a list of truly scary places ... want to see them? How brave of you! All right, I'll take you to the ten most dangerous places in the world! But before we get started, here's a little game! At the bottom of the page you will find the names of our destinations; try to guess their spot on the list and write each name next to the number you think is correct. **READ THE BOOK TO FIND OUT HOW MANY YOU GOT RIGHT!**

1 _ _ _ _ _ _ _ _ _ _ _ _ _ _ _ _ _ _

2 _ _ _ _ _ _ _ _ _ _ _ _ _ _ _ _ _ _

3 _ _ _ _ _ _ _ _ _ _ _ _ _ _ _ _ _ _

4 _ _ _ _ _ _ _ _ _ _ _ _ _ _ _ _ _ _

5 _ _ _ _ _ _ _ _ _ _ _ _ _ _ _ _ _ _

6 _ _ _ _ _ _ _ _ _ _ _ _ _ _ _ _ _ _

7 _ _ _ _ _ _ _ _ _ _ _ _ _ _ _ _ _ _

8 _ _ _ _ _ _ _ _ _ _ _ _ _ _ _ _ _ _

9 _ _ _ _ _ _ _ _ _ _ _ _ _ _ _ _ _ _

10 _ _ _ _ _ _ _ _ _ _ _ _ _ _ _ _ _ _

- LAKE NATRON
- DASHT-E LUT
- DANAKIL

- KOMODO ISLAND
- STEAMBOAT GEYSER
- BLUE HOLE DAHAB

- DARVAZA CRATER
- KAWAH IJEN
- SKELETON COAST
- ANTARCTICA

10 SKELETON COAST

LENGTH: 310 mi (500 km)
WIDTH: 25 mi (40 km)

At first glance, there doesn't appear to be anything strange about this **VERY LONG BEACH** overlooking the Atlantic Ocean. But, if you look closer, you'll notice something that makes it distinctly creepy: thousands of **BONES** and **SKELETONS** scattered across the sand.

They are the remains of the many **WHALES** and marine animals that have beached themselves over the years. This beach is actually a **DESERT**, without a single drop of fresh water. It is not unusual to see predators roaming the sands for food, scavenging among the **WRECKAGE** of the numerous ships that have fallen victim to the strong sea currents.

CONTINENT:
Africa
NATIONS:
Angola and Namibia

TYPE OF PLACE:
beach

DANGEROUS FEATURE
The presence of predators in
the area (hyenas, leopards,
and cheetahs) and the lack
of fresh water.

FUN FACT
Due to the large number of
shipwrecks, this coast is also
known as the "ship cemetery."

ANCIENT LEGEND OR REALITY?

The **DANGER** of certain places has transformed into legend and, although the shroud of **MYSTERY** surrounding them has long been unveiled, their names continue to **AWAKEN AN ANCIENT FEAR WITHIN US**.

I'm ready to investigate! How about you?

The Bermuda Triangle

The Bermuda Triangle refers to an area of the Atlantic Ocean that is found between Bermuda, Florida, and Puerto Rico. For years, there were tales of ships and planes that attempted passage through this area only to **MYSTERIOUSLY DISAPPEAR** into thin air, but not before announcing that there was a problem with their compass. There haven't been any new cases of this for a long time.

It is also known as the Devil's Triangle.

Most modern experts do not think the number of accidents in the Triangle is any higher than that of any other region with a similar volume of air and sea traffic.

The Pillars of Hercules

The promontories of the Strait of **GIBRALTAR**, connecting the Mediterranean Sea to the Atlantic Ocean, were identified in Greek mythology as "the Pillars of Hercules."

They were once considered the edge of the world, beyond which mankind could not venture.

According to Plato, beyond the Pillars of Hercules lies the legendary island of Atlantis.

The three capes

Cape Horn

Many years ago, the legend of the **THREE GREAT CAPES** was born. Over the centuries, many sailors lost their lives circumnavigating the Cape of Good Hope in Africa, Cape Leeuwin in Australia, and Cape Horn in South America. These three places are where **THE OCEANS COLLIDE WITH BRUTAL FORCE**.

The gigantic waves and strong winds make navigation very difficult, even to this day.

STEAMBOAT GEYSER

NUMBER OF ACTIVE GEYSERS IN YELLOWSTONE:
more than 200

What a "hothead"! Ha ha, get it?

This geothermal feature at **YELLOWSTONE NATIONAL PARK** is actually one of the world's most **DANGEROUS** tourist attractions. Not only is Steamboat Geyser still active, it is also the **TALLEST GEYSER IN THE WORLD**, throwing jets of water and steam more than 295 feet (90 meters) into the air. It can "wake up" at any time, when you least expect it. If you want to visit, you must absolutely stay on the marked trails, or you might accidentally **SINK INTO THE GROUND** and burn your **FEET** in the boiling groundwater, which can reach over 248°F (120°C).

CONTINENT:
North America
NATION:
United States

TYPE OF PLACE:
geothermal area

DANGEROUS FEATURE
May emit unpredictable jets of steam, and the groundwater is boiling hot.

FUN FACT
The water eruptions can last up to 40 minutes, while the subsequent jets of steam can go on for days.

AN UNDERGROUND THREAT

VOLCANOES are an unpredictable and uncontrollable force of nature. Their activity can sometimes have **DEVASTATING** effects. Eruptions can be explosive and have even released energy that is **500 TIMES STRONGER THAN AN ATOMIC BOMB**.

Explosive volcanoes

One of the most devastating volcanoes in history was **MOUNT TAMBORA**, in Indonesia, which erupted in 1815 with explosions, white-hot lava jets, toxic gases, and burning clouds, destroying the region and decimating the population. Almost 70 years later, Indonesia suffered the violent explosion of **KRAKATOA** as well.

KRAKATOA has an explosive personality!

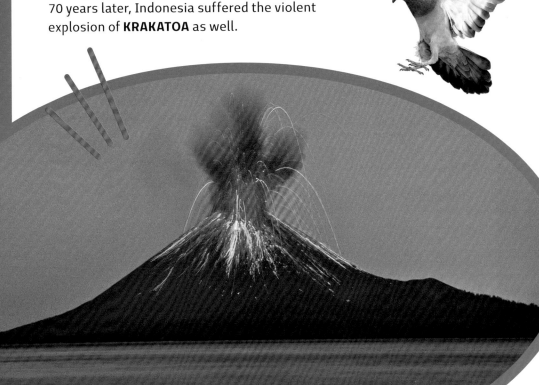

Volcanoes with lots of lava

Many volcanoes, like those in **HAWAII**, produce large quantities of lava, letting it flow away without exploding. However, if the amount of lava becomes excessive, the situation can still be very **DANGEROUS**.

During the last eruption of KILAUEA, the population was evacuated due to the risk of toxic fumes.

Underwater volcanoes and tsunamis

Where underwater volcanoes are concerned, the real **DANGER** comes from the sea! A large underwater eruption can actually cause a **TSUNAMI**. These are **ABNORMALLY LARGE WAVES** that move at unusually high speeds and crash onto the shore with disastrous effects.

On January 15, 2022, at the bottom of the Pacific Ocean, the eruption of the Hunga Tonga-Hunga Ha'apai volcano created enormous waves that reached the coast of Japan as well as the Americas.

LAKE NATRON

ALTITUDE:
1,970 ft (600 m)
MAXIMUM DEPTH:
10 ft (3 m)

Hey, wait a minute...
Those pink dots in the
lake are flamingos!
Hi there, cousins!

Its unusual **RED** color makes this a unique and splendid lake, but this beauty can also be **DEADLY**: beware of swimming! Its salty water can reach a **TEMPERATURE OF 140°F (60°C)** and is extremely corrosive. This lake's menacing nature is caused by a nearby **VOLCANO**, which erupts with extremely **TOXIC** lava. Animals that fall into the water often get stuck there and are slowly encrusted with a hard shell similar to stone, transforming them into **MUMMIES**.

CONTINENT:
Africa
NATION:
Tanzania

TYPE OF PLACE:
lake

DANGEROUS FEATURE
Lake Natron is composed of extremely salty water and is almost as corrosive as ammonia.

FUN FACT
One of the very few animals capable of living in this lake is the flamingo, which can be found here in the thousands.

BLUE HOLE DAHAB

LENGTH OF THE TUNNEL THAT LEADS TO THE OPEN SEA:
85 ft (26 m)

Wow! It's really deep!

Exploring the seabed is always an adventure, but here it can become a **HAZARD**. This natural **ABYSS** is hundreds of feet deep and is surrounded by a beautiful coral reef. It sits in the middle of the sea like a huge **CIRCULAR HOLE** with a bright blue color.

Unfortunately, it can also be a **DEATH TRAP** for divers who go too deep.

It's very easy to **LOSE YOUR SENSE OF DIRECTION**, making it impossible to find your way out.

CONTINENT:
Africa
NATION:
Egypt

TYPE OF PLACE:
submarine sinkhole

DANGEROUS FEATURE
It's a trap for divers trying to cross the underwater tunnel.

FUN FACT
Its waters are full of beautiful tropical fish.

UNDERWATER FORCES

The oceans are constantly **MOVING**, sometimes with inconceivable strength, across the whole planet.
They are driven by strong **CURRENTS** that transfer energy through the **WAVES**, and their levels go up and down every day thanks to the **TIDES**.

The movement of the oceans can be dangerous!

Giant waves

Every surfer loves a **GIANT WAVE**, but it's certainly **SCARY** when one crashes over you. Some of the largest waves can be found in **PEAHI**, on Maui, one of the Hawaiian Islands. It has been nicknamed **JAWS** because the waves, which can be more than 60 feet (18 meters) high, can be unpredictably dangerous, just like the jaws of a **SHARK**.

A tsunami (an abnormal wave created by an earthquake deep under the water) can reach 435 mph (700 km/h).

The highest point of a wave is called the crest.

Unexpected tides

There are places where the tides suddenly rush in or withdraw much faster than expected. **ZIPOLITE** beach in Mexico, for example, is also known as the **BEACH OF DEATH**. A relaxing swim here can suddenly turn into a nightmare when the water **QUICKLY WITHDRAWS**, dragging everything along with it.

In extreme situations it is almost impossible for swimmers to reach the shores in time to save themselves.

Tides are determined by the moon's gravitational pull on Earth.

Inescapable currents

UNDERWATER CURRENTS are often a trap for those enjoying a swim. People can get caught in the middle of one and be swept away without even realizing what's happened. One of the most dangerous examples can be found on the beautiful Hanakapiai Beach on the Hawaiian island of Kauai. Unfortunately, there is no way to protect yourself against the current, which can carry you more than 6 miles (10 km) away.

In ancient times it was believed that whirlpools or vortices were created by sea monsters.

Currents run through all the oceans, connecting them together.

ALTITUDE:
1,970 ft (600 m)

This SULFUR really smells!

All volcanoes have certain dangerous features, but **KAWAH IJEN** has even more than usual! In addition to **LAVA**, it constantly erupts **SULFUROUS** gas. These vapors are terribly **STINKY** and very **TOXIC**, making the air unbreathable. Anyone wishing to visit the summit has to wear a **GAS MASK** to avoid death by asphyxiation. Inside the crater you can admire a beautiful turquoise lake, but that color doesn't come from water. It's actually full of poisonous **HYDROCHLORIC ACID**.

CONTINENT:
Asia
NATION:
Java, Indonesia

TYPE OF PLACE:
volcano

DANGEROUS FEATURE
This volcano doesn't only emit toxic gases, it is also topped by a lake of acid.

FUN FACT
At night you can see the flicker of blue flames, created by the sulfur gases as they catch fire.

SURFACE AREA:
243 mi²
(391 km²)

> Yikes!
> I'll just be hiding
> over here, okay?

Landing on this island means entering the territory of one of the largest and most aggressive reptiles in the world! The **KOMODO DRAGON** has a prehistoric appearance, weighs over 220 pounds (100 kilograms), and can reach a length of 10 feet (3 meters). Its massive body doesn't prevent it from moving with **EXTREME SPEED**, and it attacks any living thing that can be turned into food. Its bite is 5 times more powerful than ours, and it is considered one of the most fearsome predators of the animal kingdom because it can inflict very serious wounds or even **DEATH**.

CONTINENT:
Asia
NATION:
Indonesia

TYPE OF PLACE:
island

DANGEROUS FEATURE
The dragon's saliva contains a substance that prevents blood from clotting, so the victim continues to bleed long after the bite.

FUN FACT
As long as you avoid the large reptiles, Komodo is a lovely place! Its most famous beach is pink, thanks to tiny fragments of red coral mixed into the white sand.

VERY DANGEROUS WILDLIFE!

Surely you CAN't be talking about me!

Sometimes a place can be dangerous because of the **LETHAL ANIMALS** living there, ready to **ATTACK** humans.

The slithering island

Snake Island in Brazil is an island full of **SNAKES WITH A DEADLY BITE**. The island is so dangerous that the Brazilian authorities have closed it to the public and only a few people are allowed to set foot on it.

There are thousands of golden lancehead pit vipers, one of the most venomous species of snake.

No one lives here except for snakes!

Get out of the water!

Many beaches in South Africa are dangerous because of sharks, but **GANSBAAI BEACH** is on another level. The whole stretch of coast has earned the title of **GREAT WHITE SHARK CAPITAL OF THE WORLD.**

Sharks come very close to the shore.

The greatest threat to sharks? That would be human beings!

Watch out for bears!

Forget about cuddly little teddy bears when you're talking about polar bears! These ice lords of the Arctic Circle are actually the largest land **PREDATORS** in the world. Encounters with humans are increasing over time with **FATAL** consequences, especially when the bear is scared or **HUNGRY**.

Polar bears are the most carnivorous bear species.

They have black skin to absorb the sun's heat.

Danger in the waves

In the coastal waterways around the city of Darwin in Australia live numerous saltwater crocodiles. These **AGGRESSIVE ANIMALS** move with ease even in the water, where they are responsible for numerous **ATTACKS**.
If you ever find yourself in the area, you're better off taking a dip in a pool...

This reptile holds the record for the most powerful bite ever registered!

The saltwater crocodile is the largest reptile in the world.

 4 DASHT-E LUT DESERT

SURFACE AREA:
about 20,000 mi² (51,800 km²)

This desert is hot enough to make my feathers fall off!

Here you might feel like you're inside a **HOT OVEN**! The **EXTREME HEAT** combined with the lack of rain makes this desert particularly inhospitable.

The only things in abundance are sand and hot gravel. Visiting this place requires not only great **COURAGE** but also plenty of food, water, fuel, and anything else you might need for your trip because **NOT A LIVING SOUL** can be found here.

In the summer of 2005, this place achieved the record-setting temperature of 159.3°F (70.7°C).

CONTINENT:
Asia
NATION:
Iran

TYPE OF PLACE:
desert

DANGEROUS FEATURE
The heat here is extreme
and suffocating.

FUN FACT
In the local language, the word
"LUT" means "bare and empty."

EXTREME HEAT!

What are the hottest places on Earth?
If you're thinking of deserts, you're right.
Not only are they dry, they're almost always
exceptionally hot, sometimes even scorching.

**SOME OF THEM REACH TEMPERATURES THAT
ARE TRULY EXTREME; DEHYDRATION AND HEAT
STROKE ARE FREQUENT AND FATAL.**

Ouch! Ow!
Hot!

Death Valley

DEATH VALLEY, in the Mojave Desert of
California, has truly earned its name. The
SEARING AIR makes breathing difficult,
and the absence of drinking water is a real
problem for anyone venturing across it.

As if that
wasn't enough,
it is also home
to numerous
rattlesnakes
who make this
place even more
dangerous.

Badlands

The Australian continent is known for its wild nature, but also for its very hot and dry climate.

The region of Queensland is home to the **BADLANDS**—literal "bad lands"—which are among the **MOST INHOSPITABLE** and **DRIEST** areas in Australia. The sun's rays overheat the soil, and temperatures easily get above 140°F (60°C).

One of the few animals able to survive in this scorching climate is the Taipan, the most venomous snake in the world!

Flaming mountains

The **FLAMING MOUNTAINS** near the Chinese city of Turpan are no joke when it comes to heat! At certain times of day, under the **SCORCHING SUN**, the wind-eroded slopes really do seem to "**BURN**" like **BLAZING FLAMES**, with shades of red, orange, and yellow, depending on the light.

In summer, the temperature can easily spike to 158°F–176°F (70°C–80°C).

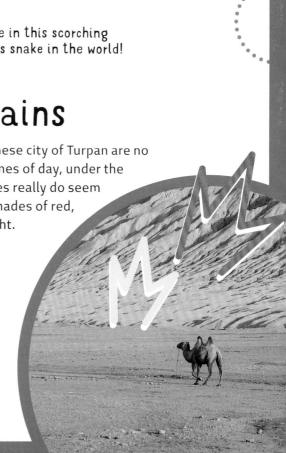

NUMBER 3 ANTARCTICA

ALTITUDE:
5.5 million sq miles
(14.2 million sq k)

Brrrr, it's cold!

Antarctica is the continent surrounding the South Pole. It is almost entirely covered in ice and snow, and you can probably guess that this place is extremely **COLD**. But can you guess exactly how cold? In the center of **ANTARCTICA**, the frozen plateau will truly test your ability to resist freezing to death. Here, winter temperatures can drop to **-144°F** (-98°C), freezing conditions that have never been reached anywhere else on Earth. A coat definitely won't be enough to protect you from the chill!

 CONTINENT:
Antarctica

 TYPE OF PLACE:
polar ice cap

DANGEROUS FEATURE
The air is incredibly dry, and each breath of air instantly transforms into icy needles.

FUN FACT
There is very little rainfall each year, so from this perspective, Antarctica can actually be considered a desert!

FROZEN WITH FEAR

In the land of **ICE**, the freezing air burns exposed skin and every breath seems to pierce the throat like hundreds of needles. The extreme cold **FREEZES THE BLOOD** in your veins and cuts right through your clothes, straight to the bone.

THE DANGER OF DEATH IN THESE PLACES IS EXCEPTIONALLY HIGH, BUT STRANGE AS IT MAY SEEM, HUMANS HAVE STILL MANAGED TO BUILD VARIOUS RESEARCH STATIONS HERE.

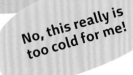

No, this really is too cold for me!

Instant snow!

In places like this, you can simply throw some water into the air to create your own **INSTANT SNOW**!

Once the water droplets make contact with the cold air they immediately **FREEZE**, creating a "fountain" of snow crystals.

In very cold winds of -17°F (-27°C), even exposed skin can freeze in less than 30 minutes.

Brave meteorologists!

Work is difficult for meteorologists at the **EUREKA** research base on **ELLESMERE** Island in the Arctic Circle. This is where they record the lowest temperatures in the entire Canadian territory. On top of that, from mid-October to late February, **THE SUN NEVER RISES** and the station spends 24 hours a day immersed in **TOTAL DARKNESS**.

The coldest village in the world

1,000 people live here.

The village of **OYMYAKON**, in Siberia, is considered the coldest inhabited place in the world. During the **VERY LONG WINTER**, inhabitants must survive powerful **POLAR WINDS** and severe temperatures that often fall below -76°F (-60°C).

2 DANAKIL DESERT

ALTITUDE:
-328 ft (-100 m)
(it's below sea level)

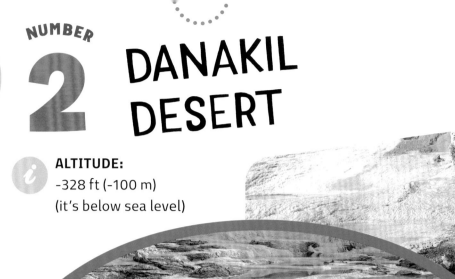

This is no ordinary desert. In addition to an air temperature that rarely falls below 122°F (50°C), this region is also a **VOLCANIC AREA** with plenty of **EARTHQUAKES**. The many iridescently colored hot springs release **SULFUR VAPORS** into the air that are particularly smelly, acidic, and **POISONOUS**. These vapors, and other highly toxic gases, render the air unbreathable and make this uninhabited place one of the **SCARIEST IN THE WORLD**. A trip here, even a short one, will definitely put your health at risk.

CONTINENT:
Africa
NATION:
Ethiopia

TYPE OF PLACE:
desert

DANGEROUS FEATURE
It releases toxic gases
and reaches exceptionally
high temperatures.

FUN FACT
This region contains one
of the most active volcanoes
in the world, Erta Ale.

1 DARVAZA CRATER

DIAMETER OF THE CRATER:
230 ft (70 m)

Be careful not to fall in!

This crack in Earth's crust in the **KARAKUM** Desert really does seem to lead to the **UNDERWORLD**, which is why the locals know it as the **DOOR TO HELL**. The **DANGER** level here is very high. It is actually a huge natural deposit of **METHANE** gas, the opening of which is as large as a soccer field. To prevent the gas from leaking into the atmosphere, it was set on fire in 1971, and it has burned uninterrupted ever since!

CONTINENT:
Asia
NATION:
Turkmenistan

TYPE OF PLACE:
gaseous crater

DANGEROUS FEATURE
The crater is ready to explode at any moment.

FUN FACT
At night, the light emanating from the crater can be seen from miles away.

DANGEROUS QUESTIONS

TRY TO ANSWER THESE QUESTIONS.
DON'T BE AFRAID OF MAKING MISTAKES; JUST TURN
THE PAGE TO READ THE CORRECT ANSWER!

1- WHAT FEATURE MAKES THE SKELETON COAST EVEN MORE FRIGHTENING?

A Frequent earthquakes

B There's usually lots of thick fog

C Growing plants

2- WHAT CAUSES A GEYSER TO ERUPT?

A Water vapor

B The pull of the moon

C Vegetation

3- WHICH ANIMALS ARE ABLE TO SURVIVE ON THE SHORES OF LAKE NATRON?

A Baboons

B Flamingos

C Salamanders

4- THE BLUE HOLE IS FOUND IN THE GULF OF AQABA, WHICH TAKES ITS NAME FROM...?

A A mosque

B A king

C A city

5- WHAT IS THE MAIN SOURCE OF WORK FOR PEOPLE LIVING ON THE KAWAH IJEN VOLCANO?

A Mining

B Animal farming

C Agriculture

6- WHAT'S THE BEST WAY TO RUN FROM A KOMODO DRAGON?

A Uphill

B Zigzag

C Backward

7- THE DASHT-E LUT DESERT IS FAMOUS FOR ITS KALUTS. WHAT ARE THEY?

A Small bugs

B Local people

C Rock formations

8- IN ADDITION TO THE COLD, WHAT OTHER DISTINCTIVE TRAIT IS TYPICAL OF ANTARCTICA?

A Heavy snowfall

B Violent sea storms

C Strong winds

9- WHAT IS THE ALTITUDE OF THE DANAKIL DESERT?

A -394 ft (-120 m)

B 0 (sea level)

C 3,280 ft (1,000 m)

10- WHAT CREATED THE DARVAZA CRATER?

A Soil erosion

B An accident

C An earthquake

DANGEROUS ANSWERS

1, B
This beach is the meeting point between the icy ocean and the desert. The temperature difference between the two environments creates fog.

2, A
Rainwater filters through the earth and penetrates deep into the ground, where it comes into contact with magma-heated rocks. This creates lots of steam, generating the explosive force.

3, B
Flamingos can live in the corrosive and boiling water of the lake thanks to their hard skin and scaly legs, making them resistant to burns.

4, C
Aqaba is the only city in Jordan overlooking the gulf.

5, A The volcano has numerous sulfur mines, and the locals risk their lives every day to extract the mineral.

6, B These reptiles can only run in a straight line. If you run in a zigzag, they will soon give up the pursuit.

7, C The kalut are formations created by the wind , which shapes rock, sand, and salt.

8, C Antarctica is the windiest continent. The wind in some places can reach 199 mph (320 km/h).

9, A Danakil is found in a depression of Earth's crust below sea level.

10, B The crater was formed as a result of a drilling accident that caused the ceiling of an underlying gas cave to collapse.

CRISTINA BANFI

After graduating with a degree in natural sciences from the University of Milan, Cristina has taught in various schools. For more than 20 years, she has worked in scientific communication and educational play and has enjoyed several editorial experiences in both scholastic and educational fields, particularly those dedicated to a young audience. In recent years she has created several titles for White Star.

PHOTO CREDITS

Kurit afshen/Shutterstock: cover bottom right; Bauer Scott/Shutterstock: 16 bottom; Bergwitz Uwe/Shutterstock: 23 bottom; BiniClick/Shutterstock: 26 bottom; Bischoff Lukas Photograph/Shutterstock: 4, 4-5; I Gede Budiwijaya/Shutterstock: back cover bottom, 20; Corlaffra/Shutterstock: 7 bottom; Dawn Crystal Photography/Getty Images: 17 bottom; Delimont Danita Shutterstock: 13 right bottom; Deni_Sugandi/Shutterstock: 10 bottom; Drakuliren/Shutterstock: 3, 34; Efendy Ada/Shutterstock: 18-19; Allen.G/Shutterstock: 11 bottom; Gasich Tatiana/Shutterstock: 31 bottom; Goinyk Production/Shutterstock: back cover bottom left, 28-29, 37 center bottom; GUDKOV ANDREY/Shutterstock: 20-21; Hedien Laura/Shutterstock: 8-9; Isselee Eric/Shutterstock: 28; Iwanami Photos/Shutterstock: 35 bottom right; Kichigin/Shutterstock: 6 bottom; lexrvulescu/Shutterstock: cover bottom left; Lockenes/Shutterstock: 1 bottom right, 37 bottom left; Manamana/Shutterstock: 32; Szymczak Marcin/Shutterstock: 25 bottom; Marketa1982/Shutterstock: 14-15, 36 bottom right; May Boyle Katie/Shutterstock: 7 bottom; Kate_N/Shutterstock: 9 bottom right, 36 center; Zheltiakov Pavel/Shutterstock: 27 bottom; Photomaster/Shutterstock: 6 bottom, 8, 12; Piu_Piu/Shutterstock: 30 bottom; Borovka Radek/Shutterstock: 32-33; Rehak Matyas/Shutterstock: cover bottom, 34-35; Restimage/Shutterstock: 26 bottom, 40; F. Rubino/Shutterstock: 27 bottom; Uryadnikov Sergey/Shutterstock: 22 bottom, 37 center bottom; Shuai Jie Guo/Shutterstock: 14; Smarta/Shutterstock: 19 bottom right; Solarisys/Shutterstock: 15 bottom right; Stockphoto mania/Shutterstock: 16 bottom, 20 left, 22 bottom, 24, 36 bottom left, 37 bottom right; Stringer/Getty Images: 11 bottom; Larina Vera/Shutterstock: 12-13; Wirestock Creators/Shutterstock: 1 bottom left, 22 center; Wolfgang Kaehler/Getty Images: 31 bottom right, 31 center; Mrs_ya/Shutterstock: 10 bottom, 18, 30 bottom, 37 bottom; Andrey Yurlov/Shutterstock: back cover bottom right, 23 bottom; Birukov Yury/Shutterstock: 24-25.

Design and layout: Valentina Figus

WS whitestar kids™ is a trademark of White Star s.r.l.

© 2024 White Star s.r.l.
Piazzale Luigi Cadorna, 6 - 20123 Milan, Italy
www.whitestar.it

Translation: Qontent
Editing: Michele Suchomel-Casey

First printing, May 2024

ISBN 978-88-544-2101-1
1 2 3 4 5 6   28 27 26 25 24

Printed and manufactured in China
by XY Cultural and Creative Park, Guangzhou